In Light and Shadow

A collection of our best poetry

Charly and Elizabeth Wood

ERETE'S BLOOM
Gaston ꙮ Cherry Grove
Oregon
2014

Copyright© by ERETE'S BLOOM
All rights reserved

For information about permission to reproduce selections from this book, email **eddi47patt@gmail.com**

1st Edition

ISBN: 13: 978-0615968865

Printed in the United States of America

The following poems are published here for the first time:
Snake, Pit Bull, Oedipus Reflects, Pun ctuation, If You Go, Wolf Man, Bananas, That Old Time Religion, She Was Looking for It, Mother's Day

Poems previously published: *Marking Time* (**Poetry Motel**), *Ceramic Vision* (**Black Hammock Review**) *Moon in Wane* (**Red Owl Press**), *High Death* (**Sandcutters**) *Forgetting* (**South Ash Press**) *Wood Ears, Payman's Fire, Where Angels Drown, and Coyote* (**Open 24 Hrs**), *Franky* (**The Darker Musings**), *Mother's Horses, Mindstorm,* and *Chai Na Kurda,* (**The Laughing Dog**)

Dedication

To the memories of
my beloved husband Charly
my beloved mother Libby
and

Our Mentor of the Tucson Poetry Workshop
Will Inman

Two Horses block print on rice paper by Libby Boyt, 1950

If you bring forth what is in you
what you bring forth will save you.
If you do not bring forth what is within you
what you do not bring forth will destroy you.
     —The Gospel of Thomas

Forward

The creation of yet another poetry book for public reading is an act of incalculable idiocy. A book of poetry created by two people, shoulder to shoulder tied page by page, is nothing short of miraculous. And yet every simple page, like a day, is its own miracle. Art is made at every moment the creator picks up the tools of life to make, fashion, dream, revise, and reflect. Between pain and ease; suffering and comfort; longing and fulfillment; humor and despair; loneliness and companionship—between the light and the shadow we all share—what we have written comes to you. We give our living into the words, and in return, when you read them and let them dance light and shadow across your own being, the words return life to us.

In this book, Charly's poems appear to left, and Elizabeth's to right. The poems (written during a period of between 1996 and 2007) support one another at each opening of the book just as we might appear hand in hand together before All that Is.

Contents

SNAKE	PIT BULL
THAT OLD TIME RELIGION	CHAI NA KURDA
SHE WAS LOOKING FOR IT	CERAMIC VISION
OEDIPUS REFLECTS	HIGH DEATH

FRANKY

MOTHER'S HORSES

WOLF MAN	MOON IN WANE
BANANAS	FORGETTING
IF YOU GO	PAYMAN'S FIRE
MOTHER'S DAY	WHERE ANGELS DROWN
PUN CTUATION	MARKING TIME
MINDSTORM	WOOD EARS
COYOTE	PINE DRAGON

SNAKE

I was the serpent in the Garden,
much maligned, me; no *miching malhecho*.
I saw myself--reflected in the silvery waters
of Gihon--as the messenger of truth, or even,
on a mission from God to correct one of his white lies.
He so oft says things he doesn't mean, like
   . . . the day that thou eatest thereof thou shalt surely die.
(as it turned out they didn't, you know)
when he showed them the tree of knowledge of good and evil.

Why would he do that? Well, he is a jealous god,
was not prepared to put up with Adam and Eve forever,
that's what I think; he didn't talk about the tree of life, that
would have made them like him forever.

He told me that too; about the knowledge tree.
I ate that apple anyway and the truth set me free,
then I knew what to do--
I ate the other fruit, the good one from the tree of life
and that's when I learned what eternity meant.

And then, happy with thoughts of living forever,
while wound relaxing amid all the branches of knowledge
had the disturbing thought.
If Adam and Eve died I would be alone with God again, a
terrible bore, his talking about his work.

Adam and Eve were more fun, though children
short-lived, and as yet short attention spans.
But, world-making thought,
if I could feed them the apple of knowing,
they too would eat from the tree of life.

We could be playmates, friends forever.

PIT BULL

I have one, see, sitting outside
bone white and chained to a post
Next to the corner of my storage room.
It is the vigilant agent
of my neighbor's territorial protection.
We have not come together yet
To share heart; and may never be able to.

Often I watch the dog sit in its muddy space of a low
Slung grey winter day, hunched over on a small
Square of wood with its back to the wind.
Oh, I understand, really I do—
This isn't a safe part of town, here
Where I've come to live a refugee
From the oppressions of middle-class smugness
And suburban home associations. Just
Give me one good, healthy all-American
Out in the open crazy but very quiet, shambled,
Mixed blood small-town block any day
To the look down the nose sounds of rider
Lawn mowers and high-powered leaf blowers.

Except for the dog. It barks.
There's no fence except its bark to divide
What's mine from what's his.
And after all, it is a pit bull, not a Chihuahua.
So too often I imagine, what if it slipped its chain one time
And I, or even more deliciously horrible, a child--
Fell even from my own back yard into its jaws.
I've heard stories;   run them at night,

When the dog turns into one of those middle of the dark
Chest-sitting nightmares, with its haunches curled
Under its gut against the cold and all its hungry backbone
Knobs sticking out in blind fury. You know, the kind
That won't move as long as you don't breathe. . .

THAT OLD TIME RELIGION

Where was the god of love when we sat in the upper room--
Sad sweet voices singing below--
And in hard and narrow chairs were so taught terror
Fear spasms yet the years and touches me?

I loved the preacher's wife,
Spare little sparrow, upright and tight,
(Did she ever in her long life smile?)
Admired her then as wise,
Pity now her faithful folly.

I feared the preacher--up on stage, sweating, jumping,
Working his trade in the spiritual spotlight--
From our mind's depths raising hell every Sunday.
And making us knaves watch it burn in the apse,
Four dimensional blood and Dolby shrieks, clear across the decades.

Now I wonder at all a life's energy spent to evoke airy vanities,
A god and his chosen, who hated and killed all not them
(me for one, but all beyond a patch of promised dirt).
Is there no god of Love in all of time and places
Bigger than a nutshell and broader than a one-toned soul?

If not, who manufactured tenderness
And lone thoughts that summon joyous tears?

CHAI NA KURDA   JANG NA KARDA
(If you don't drink tea, you can't wage war)

"Your father called.
I told him you were asleep."
Silence eddied in the wake
of my daughter's pass through the living room.
I brewed breakfast chai, forcing myself to allow the fist
of that which is now continue beating what once
was further back into her past unimpeded. attempts
To soften only bruises the wound.
She sighed on a turn of teenage ramble, then sank
by the window, where loose strands of dark hair
ignited into a late-morning summer blonde.
Delicately vigilant, I poured the brown liquid thickly swirled
into a reality turned mutable, unstable, and rudely
sweetened.
Handing her the cup, I wished I could unhand her the war
That there is only one particular strain of enduring
strength gained through irreparable loss.
But she looked up with stretched pleasure
in the bitter drink and said with simple relief,
"Thank you for not waking me."

"SHE WAS LOOKING FOR   IT"

"It" is an indefinite pronoun.

If a woman approaches a man,
Or allows a man to approach her,
Certainly she was looking for "it,"
But for her "it" is "that."

She might be willing to give "it" to get "that."
But chances are "it" was not "that,"
and definitely, that was not it.

What was that? No, "that" was not "it."
She wanted "that" but he offered "it."
She told him she might come to want "it,"
but for right now all she wanted was "that."

He wasn't sure he had that
and began to wonder about it.
He had plenty of "it," and
He used to get "it," but he never gave "that."

At least he didn't think so as "that" was . . .
He didn't know what.
Could it be "what" she really wanted?
No, not that, she said.

But she had said she <u>wanted</u> "that,"
And he was pretty sure he was losing it.

The trouble with men is that they have such short

vocabularies.

CERAMIC VISION

What I was before You
Held me in Your hands
I do not know, but by Your touch I have
Learned to love You, Beautiful Shaper.
Deep into the heavy dross
Of my formless being Your
Hands speak, and by them,
Defined, I grow round-swirled
Until moist dialogue rises; my flat scent
Filling Your lungs.
Under Your hand's heel I warp
And stretch, elastic pulled
Into the form-desire of Your creating heart.
Sweeter than water is the firm curl
Of Your thumb along my rim
Where I am summoned to sing
The long songs of possibility.
Then let the tips of Your delicate
Fingers ridge my sides into breath,
Slow and even where lies the eagerness
Of the unborn to manifest.
By You I am made into this bowl,
Hollowed and burned into such full,
Impregnated silences
As could bind Us.

OEDIPUS REFLECTS

That old man I killed along the narrow road,
Nothing to me then, why do I dream of him now?
A fair fight for mere right of way,
A rite of passage for me. He died.

Every night he returns, blind to reality and necessity,
He comes serene-eyed, to renew our lengthened battle.
In dreams I stare at his face and wonder who he was.

What was he to me that I should weep for him?
Just an old man astride the road, blocking my way.
I had far to go and little time, and besides,
It is nature that the young should kill the old.

How dare this dark nothing invade my dreams each night
Not with anger but like a loving traveler returning home?

HIGH DEATH

Easy comfort in loamy,
Well-chewed soils could
Not hold me. Apart from
All others I took escape
From the water-rich stench
Of common rot to root
The high ground, willing
To pay the price for
Individuation and pride.
Here life clings precarious,
Thin under days of a too-
Ardent sun and nights so
Chill no dawn could thaw them.
Here years fall as stones,
Dry tears wept out of a
Mountainside, and here
No water stays whistling
Life where I am denied wilt,
Or soft collapse to the ground.
Instead, I stand drawn
Rigid, hollow and shriveled as
Scant moisture burns marrow,
Long cold claims bone, and I am carved
Into a flute for the high wind of death.

FRANKY

I met Frankenstein's Monster the other night;   Jeez!
rain, thunder, lightning, terrible wind!   Good thing
we were inside the corner bar.

Bob's Bar--not one of those fancy-named places; a good
bar that smelled,   well, pretty bad:
beer, vinyl, cigarettes, a little sweat, cologne, something
damp and a little blue-tinged--the way a bar is supposed to
smell.
Bob's had been something better once, big, with real wood
walls and now-black rafters almost visible above. Cool, a
little eerie.

The place was hollow when I went in but I was used to
emptiness.
I didn't notice when the Monster sat down across from me.

Not a bad guy, really. A little--put-offish--at first if you
know what I mean.
Well, actually even I don't know what I mean.
He wasn't ugly, like you've heard;   rough-hewn, but
otherwise sorta nondescript.

But when you looked into his eyes . . .
well, you looked away. Then back. It was like that.

Surely the son of a bitch could afford some better clothes
(I mean, clean enough, but . . .) And for God's sake stop
cutting his own hair
(chilling image, scissors glinting in bathroom mirror)
Still, in the dim bar light he looked all right. It was just that
I looked into his eyes. Had to.
You could look as deep as you wanted.
Nothing there.

I mean, he started talking and in a nearly empty place
what do you do? Move? He wasn't all <u>that</u> big, still . . .So
I talked, he talked, we talked.
He bought, I bought (he drinks stout, by the way. Figures).

Bright guy, really.
Interesting enough once I got him off existentialism--
Jesus, is that still around?--
He pronounced old Jean Paul as "sar tray,"
A man who read but never heard a lecture.

Come to think of it, I guess he wouldn't.

I understand that his wife is dead.
Called her his "bride," but later said they'd been married
20/30 years.

Lonely guy, I guess. Just needs a friend.
Not a lot of applicants, I bet.

We talked biology a bit; guess that was his thing.
Not mine. I never could understand organic stuff.
Then we got to talking about cosmology, layman quantum
stuff, No "science guy" either one of us, but he was good
on ideas,
and--real important--he listened when I talked too.
Have to admit, I was warming to the guy.

Then there was this horrendousgodawfulcrash of
lightning/thunder. <u>Under</u> the rafters I'd swear, and so close
together you thought they both came first.

He had a thing about lightning, I think.

Scared me but, big surprise, got to him worse by far;
but for a brief shining moment Bob's was daylight lit
And I realized,   shit,
I was just staring into the mirror behind the bar.

MOTHER'S HORSES

Ma, where are your horses? I've called;
"Come for sweet cracked corn, alfalfa, and warm
Safe from storms in the barn; come rest and drink a quiet water."

But she says, "My horses won't come, not
When they've gone wild to run Spring wood
Where the lace of fine green leaves and blushing petals
Shiver their hides. Curves of rippling grain
Under the barks of trees in their ancient
Seasons urge muscle to speed sheer joy of life running.
And wherever my horses pass, silent stumps
And logs lie in wait for them; crouching
Low in the dark shapes of wolves.

"A thick Summer water my horses shake slack
Rivulets and rippling ponds where
The heron's reed head lifts to keening frogs.
And then they kick a lightning fire into one another;
Running on a black storm's breath warm and quick
As the hawk dips wing--to ride
Sweet mists hurrying to join rains thirsting for the ground.

"Then, listen for Autumn's weight, where hooves
Charged with dire rhythms bring down the golden showers;
Over leaves my horses pound pulse into the ground.
And under my hands, in stone carved thin to vein
Light in their manes and tails flash--
Where they run limestone hidden caverns
The sound rolls up like the long low
Growl of a wolf's fall leaf hunger.

"And look above you; high in Winter air my horses
Rush before the lash of ice and snow. Beyond
Sun's turn from etched glass so cold the force
Of breath fills the blue sharp edge of an early dawn sky.
As hurried clouds they run, my white horses.
And in their calls there stirs a wind where
The hawk's thin cry dips wide promises of unencumbered
space."   "And you with them?"

"I am; only feel the turn of seasons through
Wild lands of living; the wood of your bones.
Your fired breath is our courage; your tears our rain.
My horses and I run your blood--always running before
your call;
Where the wolf takes my hands and feet to dance--
The white hawk my hair for wings.

WOLF MAN

Every month as the moon rounds gibbous
bounding toward full,
Begins the itching of the palms,
The jangle deep inside the knees
A tolling bell weather of the feeling he has awaited, hated,
When he becomes something he never wanted to be.
Something primal,
        something feral,
                something alien,
Something that later eludes memory

Come the moon rising full he is taken over by,
Not goodness, but godless Godness,
So alive that he cannot contain his own bonds,
Frightened at the awesome power of his soul.
Adrenal-driven down dark mental streets
Where he fears he might meet himself, he roams,
Suddenly electric-souled burning in the night.

Sunset to sunrise he lives in heart-racing terror,
In fear his soul will explode in its intensity;
Not pain, beyond pleasure, a reeling past feeling.
Moonset.   Dawn.   Ditch-awakening in the dirt of himself,
Forgetful of the night, unsure what he had felt,
Knowing he had drunk the moon's wine to the dregs,
the month ahead a long slow inhaling of stale water,
Waiting, waiting, for the full moon

Afraid, waiting.

Impatient

MOON IN WANE

For you I hunger
As the waning moon
Drips want of the sun.
Later each night more close
To reflected knowing I
Dare, until, driven desperate,
Into early morning I linger;
A ghost's wail against bird song,
A melted sweetness under
The last dreams of sleep, or
A powder thumb print thievishly
Smudged across a clear sky.
Though closer to you I lift
Yet more keen grows my need
To fill by your warm presence.
Even as pale arms reach to
Your bright aurora and clouds
Whisper soft joining,
Only want covers the round
Black of me, and fed
Emptiness, I swell dark.

BANANAS

Buying a banana is a serious thing,
A commitment to time and space,
Color--probably a middle-green--a concern,
Allocation of space first--between coffeepot
and microwave perhaps

And then of time--How soon from green to gold but not to
brown? (are a few cinnamon freckles acceptable?)
And appetite--Does one crave a banana tonight, tomorrow,
Thursday? One might want a banana right now, But can
never count on any ready-ripe bananas when on entering a
store--Track down and harass a clerk--"Do you have any
other bananas today?"

Never store in the refrigerator, of course
But some use a brown paper bag to hasten the gold--
Tricky that, requiring frequent checks, the banana no
longer visible.

Ambient room temperature at times of day or night?
Window open or closed? Prevailing wind currents?
Time of year? Fortunately tidal forces can be neglected,
And gravity can be ignored, though it's better to turn
The banana once to insure even ripening.

This for one banana. Relatively simple.

But the desire for consumption of a second banana
  (how many days apart, for example)
The problem becomes immensely complicated,
Every factor a factor of each other factor.

Still, humanly manageable.

But three bananas, factors of factors becoming infinite.
  --the dreaded "three-body problem" in physics.

You simply must have a computer to buy three bananas.

FORGETTING

Up and down the Catalina Highway he walked ten miles and more a day, going nowhere in particular and coming back, as if he'd forgotten something.
"It's Santa Claus!" my daughter cried, joyfully waving out the car window.
He never glanced her way, yet we both found comfort in the flickering appearing and vanishing of this transient fixture; this personal disaster marching slowly along the curb. In brightest sunlight he walked, head bowed. White, windswept hair and beard covered a stained jacket out of which the zipper jutted as a broken tooth.

Broad shoulders bore a backpack stuffed with days and nights of waiting, sitting in the shade of mall shops, eating meals of bread and cheese, sleeping bench-straight upon his back to be filled with star-crossed dreams. Inside the library on rainy days, we found him sitting alone, amnesia bound, tranced eyes staring at water rilling down window glass. An open book of ancient plays lay on his lap.
King Lear? Timon of Athens?

"I think I remember I used to live in California," he told us, just before he vanished.
"California?" we asked, as parts of us edged away and other parts, eager to hear the tale, sidled closer to the whisky-soothed sigh.

"Look what I found," he said, digging deep into his backpack. "Here, you keep it."

He hung the squashed sleigh bell around my daughter's neck as if she might need it to remember her way home again and I, hearing its weak, flat-tinned ring, might never lose her.

IF YOU GO . . . .

Insanity runs in all the fine old Southern families.

My sister said she just wanted to get away,
To step around the corner into peace.
But she forebore that fearful turning,
Somehow knowing that once you slip round
the corner
        you can't come back.

The old Greeks knew the meaning of Lethe,
(not a good night's sleep, etymologically a lethal
first cousin).
How pleasant to forget but if you drink
        you can't come back.

I would have drunk from the river to forget that
one hour.
How pretty, how nice, how precious to forget just
that. But I knew, somehow, that to forget is
"to pour out,"
Leaving great grey gaps, half a life empty, and
        you can't come back.

Unless those old Greeks were deranged,
My sister and I were at least as smart as horses,
Clipping sparse tender grass in a field of milkweed.
Life may be a barren pasture,
but if you jump the fence
        you can't come back.

PAYMAN'S FIRE

The woman seated next to me sighs. I look up, startled as if a piece of wood had settled in the hearth against the bottom heat.

It is only Payman in the flames of her disease. I don't look at her for to see is to ache. Her eyes glitter too bright; open so wide I wonder if I will fall into her plea for release--be conscripted into the search for any small vision she could clasp against soul
Over blind night.

We are waiting for her week's allowance of morphine. Secretly, I lick the palm of my hand, hoping for residue of powder. Inches from my arm, Payman proceeds with long slow transformation.
Her skin stretches translucent against
the press of all the time she does not have,
as the rage of cancer rolls out of her organs into
blood   fingers   nails   hair.
Inside, bones fuse, huddled children
clutching one another, terrified the next moment
may scatter them into an ossuary of oblivion.

For Payman there is neither past regret nor future anticipation; only now
This moment's joy   This instant's pain.
She keeps things simple and light because
she is too frail to carry much.
A smile passing as a breeze.
The brush of a small girl's frock
Against the side of her leg
The taste of a plum.

Later I will take her home to the darkened room where under ash
Payman glows--Her deepest need a sip of water

Her greatest task to draw   the next breath.

MOTHER'S DAY

She did not precisely die so much as slowed,

A graduated leaving.

Still, silent but for breaths, eyes open;

Breathing in long heavy loud tirings, air in, no exit sounds.

There was nothing left of her but the breathing,

Time stretching longer between each intake of little life,

Longer, longer, until we waited for the next,

Then waited for the next

Until we slowly knew we had heard the last

While waiting for the next,

Waiting that stretched into eternity.

Her final inspiration was to slip the room.

WHERE ANGELS DROWN

What wings pound at risk when the small boy is told;
when alone of all others he runs, light-pulled to throw arms
around the edges of the basin prairie, none but he can tell.
"Oh, don't you know. . .?" He says, voice drifting
silent before the curious attention of his elders.
Only a child's legs voice grass to learn it, thumping fear
into running lungs when he finds he cannot, even in a
lifetime of dreams of running, approach the rim where sky
presses ground. There, throwing himself into finite arcs
across the ancient sea bed now vanished, the boy, between
lift and fall, between muscle's surging desire and weight's
settled love, finds of himself the angel to failed chance,
accident of celestial wing; divine cry of mortal end.
That when running from having run to the end of
endurance before the edge of that vast bowl,
all he can say is,   "Don't you know? Don't you. . ."
Until what the angel whispers out
of a breath drenched with too much air
"Don't you know, Don't you know this is. . ."

Where the boy falls alone, there to find beauty's fine rage
between body's plunge and heart's ineffable song the arrow
fletched by the sun. "Don't you know,
oh, don't you know?"

Oh, you so old, and far wise
that you must shed useless wings
before descending into the sea of no mercy, oh, don't you
know this prairie, this place of all the world
as the boy tells, eyes wide with risk,
"Don't you know that THIS is where angels drown?"

PUN CTUATION
>   an English teacher's valentine

Won't you be my apostrophe,

The winkle that makes me possessive,

a turning away from the madded world?

What is the comma that separates us,

Makes us two divided logos,

The hyphen that halves us?

Erase that dieresis and we are in

Sudden conjunction.

Our instant love will explode,

In an exclamation point

Making a joyful period of the rest of our lives,

Parenthesed apart from the interrogative world.

MARKING TIME

"Before the blind horse was born,"
I say, making of that birth
A mark of time. It was an event
So striking that twenty years later
The sensation of my body bending,
Storm-pounded toward that delicately
Formed filly as she lay in the mud;
Or the touch of my disbelieving hands
Upon those unfulfilled sockets
Still trembles through my dreams.
In that long moment, alone,
Without worded comfort
That such defects were possible
I felt the knowledge rise within,
Struggled to birth justification until
At last a clean surge of rain-bound blindness
Lifted from my eyes. Since then,
In the sweep of summer storms I hear
The horse race crashing into her fence;
In each slash of lightning feel
The shock of barbed contact,
And in the rumble of thunder
Hear the fall of that black,
Unsighted body to the ground.

I had never feared such storms
Before the blind horse was born.

MIND STORM

From where this mind storm,
This freakish wind erasing reason?
Not from nil, a denying thus of will,
But from in, generations deep.
My grandfather's rage, my father's anger
Generationed down to a silent pain with me?

Is this some Darwinian progress of the psyche,
Some bettering-but-not-very-damned-much of spirit?
Is withdrawing in silent pain, a self-hurt anger,
Better than exploding in heat and light?
Perhaps to innocent bystanders, only me wounded,
but within the pressure all-taken double-agonies.

This storm does not brew from nothing
but from some slight hurt or hurting slight
from a drive-by word shooter
aiming perhaps not at me
or perhaps an aim at slighter slighting,
translated from depth to heavier artillery saying,
"You do not measure up to a man's height
breadth
depth.

It's not that I am not the man my father was.
Worse, I am the man my father was, exact measure,
and he the man my grandfather was.

How many generations does it take to grow an inch of
soul?

WOOD EARS

When trees die slowly from the inside, they die
Covered by the sounds of life, and their bark
Opens to water, air, earth, and fire.
And in those openings, trees sometimes grow ears
The way old women grow moles on double chins;
Extensions of an inner self no longer bound
By youth's crude symmetry.

Dying trees shake senescence past, and grow
Wood ears to hear all the delicate
Tiny voices of decay that lie
Shimmering on bark like a drizzle rain.
And they listen, drawing to them the sounds of life
To which their dying sends invitation:

Narrow snake vines cursed to creep along the dark,
Sad ground, surround and upward reaching closely
Twine a rotting ancient and cling still to bits of bark
The way widows hold hats close to their hearts
For the throbbing echo of the Beloved's voice.

Insects, too, add their voices through winter
day. Dreams of clustered ladybugs blanketed by
loose bark whisper, head to head, tales of sun-
warmed flights, and the soft, toe-tickling ridges
of a small child's hand.

And under all, deep between atrophied roots
there runs a river's never-ending roar; promising
one day a sparked cry will burst to suck new green
from soil compounded wood ears.

COYOTE

What did you have in mind, trickster,
That instant before I killed you?
We have too much in common not to understand.
Shit happens, Coyote,
and ages of grief will not dispel that flashing
less-than-a-moment before I destroyed you.

We have too much in common not to understand,
fellow more-than-dogs   less than wolves,
we live by our wits; act and die on a whim.

You ran safe beside me, but in a losing race,
then I think you chose to side-wind
in front of the steel horse I rode at 70 miles per hour
I think you were playing a joke,
meant to leap in front of me,
then speed ahead,
your usual trick,
leaving me in the dust,
not comprehending, coyote,
how fast a Toyota could run

died in that sudden learning.

I understand, Coyote, a trick I could have played.
Forgive me that I had only a instant to admire your beauty,
no time to avoid your prank,
time only to kill.

Smoke tobacco with me now
and we will be at an understanding
and talk   paced shoulder to shoulder
        --man to canine--
              of other tricks we have played.

PINE DRAGON

Long ago, it came to us from Thailand,
a dark green dragon made of *papier
mache* with painted scales outlined
in black. When put on the table, four
sturdy legs supported its substantial
body; clearly not the sort to go flying
to or from, but giving the air of having
thoughtfully walked through strange places,
since tiny flames suggestively curled over
its frozen joints.

Mother, whose cosmology permitted
no idleness of creatures actual or illusory, at once
gave the dragon its prestigious job of standing
at the foot of our Winter Solstice tree.

This we yearly crusted with glass hopes; whispered
bubble lights; an angel blue-gowned in plastic opened
in the back for gentle, loving silver wings;
popcorn and cranberry drops strung in blooded purity.

Across each night's heavy walk into the slighted dawn,
our dragon's vigil protected the new year's exhaling
grief before the intake of fresh expectation.
Sometimes, now old I feel myself child-curled under
its tree, shielded between what was, and what should
have been. And the time is winter; white with bitter
cold when my lungs, remembering, fill with the scent
of pine.

www.ingramcontent.com/pod-product-compliance
Lightning Source LLC
Chambersburg PA
CBHW070049070426
42449CB00012BA/3203